J 332.497 c

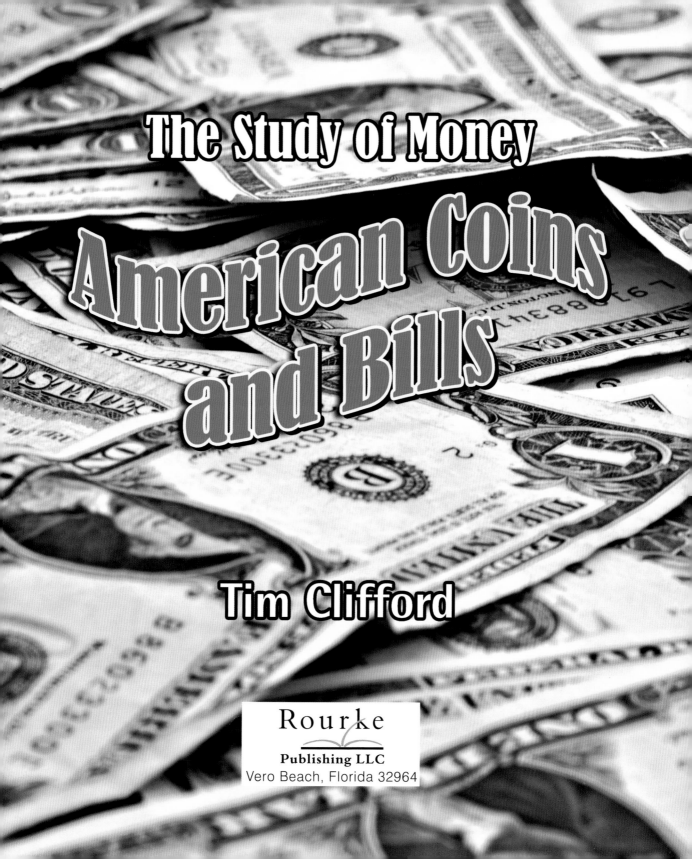

The Study of Money

American Coins and Bills

Tim Clifford

Rourke
Publishing LLC
Vero Beach, Florida 32964

www.rourkepublishing.com

PHOTO CREDITS: © Arvind Balaraman: page 4; © STILLFX: page 5, 12, ; © Sascha Burkard: page 6; © pandapaw: page 7; © NatureBoy: page 8; © RagnaRock: page 9 top; © Robynrg: page 9 bottom; © Marcus Miranda: page 10, 11; © Robert Kylio: page 13; Vova Pomortzeff: page 14, 15 top, 16 top; © Morning Palace: page 15 bottom; © United States Mint: page 16 bottom, 17 bottom, 18; © Library of Congress: page 17 top, 21; © Michael G.Smith: page 20; © Herbert Kratky: page 22; © Jon S. Sfondalias: page 23; © Frank Anusewics: page 24; © Christophe Testi: page 25; © microstocker: page 26; © Dragunov: page 27; © Alex James Bramwell: page 28; © Foto Factory: page 29; © Andresr: page 30

Editor: Jeanne Sturm

Cover Design: Renee Brady

Page Design: Tara Raymo

Library of Congress Cataloging-in-Publication Data

Clifford, Tim, 1959-
  American coins and bills / Tim Clifford.
      p. cm. -- (The study of money)
  Includes index.
  ISBN 978-1-60472-402-8
  1. Money--United States--Juvenile literature. I. Title.
  HG501.C64 2009
  332.4'973--dc22

                                2008011305

Printed in the USA

IG/IG

Table of Contents

American Currency

Everyone recognizes money when they see it, and just about everyone wants more of it! Yet we rarely stop to think what money stands for. Money is a **currency**, which means we can exchange it for goods and services. Most countries have their own currency.

In America, our currency is based on the United States dollar. The dollar is the most basic **denomination**, or amount, of money issued in the United States. Most coins come in denominations of one dollar or less. All bills, or paper money, come in denominations of one dollar or more.

The United States Dollar

The George Washington Presidential $1 Coin

The dollar was first established as the official currency of the United States in 1775. At that time, the dollar was a coin, but most of today's dollars are printed on paper.

The first paper dollar was printed in 1862. A picture of former **Treasury** Secretary Salmon P. Chase was printed on the front, or **obverse**. A picture of George Washington first appeared on the dollar bill in 1869, and his portrait is still used on the dollar today.

The United States **Mint** currently issues Presidential $1 coins. Each has a picture of a president stamped on the front.

Dollar bills used to be larger. They were first printed in their current size in 1929.

The *Great Seal* appears on the **reverse** of the bill. It shows an unfinished pyramid with an eye floating above it.

Talking about the United States Dollar

There are many ways to refer to the U.S. dollar. Here are some of the more common ways.

Symbol : $

Abbreviation: USD or US$.

Slang names for the dollar include: Greenback, Washington, Clam, Buck, and Single.

Other Paper Money

Besides the dollar, United States currency comes in other denominations, or amounts. Paper money, also known as Federal Reserve Notes, is currently printed in denominations of $1, $2, $5, $10, $20, $50, and $100. In the past, the U.S. printed larger denominations. The largest was $100,000!

Obverse side

Reverse side

The Two Dollar Bill

- Picture on Obverse: Thomas Jefferson, U.S. President
- Picture on Reverse: A painting called *The Declaration of Independence*

- Many people refuse to use the two dollar bill because they believe it can be easily confused with a five dollar bill.

The Five Dollar Bill

- Picture on Obverse: Abraham Lincoln, U.S. President
- Picture on Reverse: The Lincoln Memorial
- Nicknames: A five dollar bill is also called a fin, a fiver, or a Lincoln.

The Ten Dollar Bill

- Picture on Obverse: Alexander Hamilton, former U.S. Secretary of the Treasury
- Picture on Reverse: The U.S. Treasury Building
- Nicknames: A ten dollar bill is also called a ten spot, a sawbuck, a Hamilton, or a tenner.

The Twenty Dollar Bill

- Picture on Obverse: former U.S. President, Andrew Jackson
- Picture on Reverse: The White House
- Nicknames: A twenty dollar bill is also called a Jackson or a double sawbuck.

The Fifty Dollar Bill

- Picture on Obverse: former U.S. President, Ulysses S. Grant
- Picture on Reverse: The U.S. Capitol Building
- Nickname: A fifty dollar bill is also called a Grant.

The Hundred Dollar Bill

- Picture on Obverse: former U.S. Statesman, Benjamin Franklin
- Picture on Reverse: Philadelphia's Independence Hall
- Nicknames: A hundred dollar bill is also called a C-Note (C is the Roman numeral for 100), a Benny, or a Benjamin.

United States Coins

In United States currency, the dollar is divided into 100 cents. We use the term cent to mean 1/100th of a dollar. The symbol for cent is ¢. United States coins are currently minted in denominations of 1¢, 5¢, 10¢, 25¢, 50¢, and 100¢ (or the one dollar coin).

The Cent

Although we often call it a penny, the official name for this coin is the cent. On the obverse is a portrait of Abraham Lincoln. The Lincoln Memorial is pictured on the reverse.

Originally, cents were made entirely of copper. Over the years, the price of copper has gone up and the amount of copper in the penny has gone down. Today, the cent has less than 3 percent copper in it. The rest is made of zinc.

Did you know...

Did you know that pennies actually cost more than a penny each to make? Because of this, some people want to get rid of the cent. Still the coin remains popular, and it is due to be redesigned. It seems the penny will remain with us for a long time.

The Nickel

The value of the nickel is five cents.
- Obverse: U.S. President Thomas Jefferson
- Reverse: Monticello, Jefferson's home
- Odd fact: The nickel is only 25 percent nickel. The other 75 percent is copper.

The Dime

The value of the dime is ten cents.
- Obverse: U.S. President Franklin D. Roosevelt
- Reverse: A torch surrounded by olive branches (representing freedom)
- Odd fact: The dime is the smallest United States coin, even though it is worth more than the cent or the nickel.

The Quarter

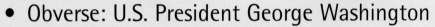

The value of the quarter is twenty-five cents, or one quarter of a dollar.

- Obverse: U.S. President George Washington
- Reverse: An eagle (prior to 1999)
- Odd fact: Since 1999, the 50 States Quarters program has produced five new quarters each year. Each new quarter has a design that represents one of the fifty states.

The Half Dollar

The value of the half dollar is fifty cents.

- Obverse: U.S. President John F. Kennedy
- Reverse: The Presidential Seal (an eagle with a shield)
- Odd fact: The eagle on the reverse is circled by fifty stars representing the fifty states. The eagle holds thirteen arrows, representing the original thirteen colonies of the United States.

15

The Dollar Coin

The value of the dollar coin is one hundred cents.

- Obverse: Sacagawea, a Shoshone Indian scout from the Lewis and Clark Expedition
- Reverse: A flying eagle
- Odd fact: The dollar coin is gold in color, but it is actually made of manganese-brass.

The Presidential $1 Coin Program

Beginning in 2007, the United States Mint began issuing new one dollar coins stamped with the faces of U.S. presidents. They are issued four per year, starting with the first four presidents (George Washington, John Adams, Thomas Jefferson, and James Madison).

16

Meet an Important Person

Susan B. Anthony

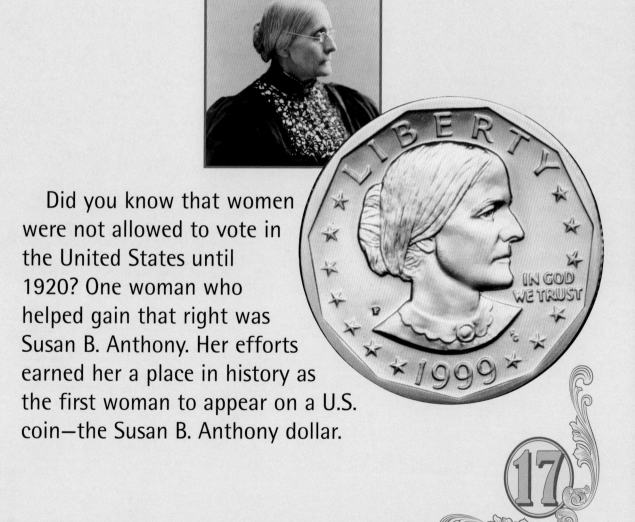

Did you know that women were not allowed to vote in the United States until 1920? One woman who helped gain that right was Susan B. Anthony. Her efforts earned her a place in history as the first woman to appear on a U.S. coin—the Susan B. Anthony dollar.

Commemorative Coins

The United States has a long tradition of **commemorating**, or honoring, people and events in its history by issuing coins. Commemorative coins are minted in small numbers. They are meant to be collected, not spent.

This coin commemorates the founding of Jamestown in 1607.

Because people buy commemorative coins but don't spend them, they help raise a lot of money. Some of this money supports the Olympics, and some helps to build **monuments** such as the Vietnam War Memorial in Washington, D.C.

The reverse of the Vietnam Veterans Memorial dollar displays the Vietnam War Service Medals.

The Department of
the Treasury

The Treasury Department has many duties, including running the Bureau of Engraving and Printing (BEP) and the United States Mint. The BEP makes all of the paper money in the U.S., and the Mint is in charge of creating all the coins.

The Treasury Department is run by the Secretary of the Treasury. Each secretary is nominated by the President and must be approved by Congress.

Meet an Important Person

Alexander Hamilton

As the first Secretary of the Treasury in United States history, Alexander Hamilton had a great deal to do with deciding how the government would collect and spend money. To honor his contributions, his picture began to appear on American money, starting back in the Civil War years. Today, his portrait is still on the ten dollar bill.

Words on Currency

We usually think of numbers when we think of money, but a lot of words also appear on United States currency.

The words *Federal Reserve Note* are printed on every bill, along with *The United States of America*. The denomination of each bill is also written in words. The statement: *This note is legal tender for all debts, public and private* means that U.S. currency must be accepted as payment for debts.

The words *In God We Trust* appear on all U.S. currency.

Coins are much smaller than bills, but they still contain some important words. Every U.S. coin has the word *Liberty* stamped on it to show how important freedom is to our country. All coins contain the United States motto *E Pluribus Unum*, which is Latin for *Out of many, one.*

Numbers on Currency

Even though money is all about numbers and counting, United States coins hardly have any numbers on them at all! The only number you'll find on a coin is the year it was minted. All other numbers are spelled out. The reverse of each coin shows its value in words, not numbers.

Date Printed

The letter code indicates where the coin was minted

Serial
Number

Date Printed

United States bills contain a lot more numbers than U.S. coins. For example, the one dollar bill contains the number *1* eight times. It appears once in each corner of the bill, on both the front and back. Other bills have a similar pattern. In addition, each bill shows the year it was produced.

Each bill also contains a serial number, which actually contains several letters as well. No two bills have the same serial number. Because of this, serial numbers can help track counterfeit or stolen money.

Counterfeit Money

It is a crime to make **counterfeit**, or fake, money, but that doesn't stop criminals from trying!

It used to be very expensive to create counterfeit money. It required an expensive printing press and engraved plates. Today, however, counterfeiters use scanners and color printers to try to make funny money that they can pass off as real.

To fight counterfeiting, the government has put a number of special features on today's money, making it harder to copy.

Today's paper money has many **security** features that make it difficult to counterfeit, such as:

- Multi-colored backgrounds
- Color-shifting ink (number in lower right-hand corner changes from green to copper depending on how it is viewed)
- A security thread that can be seen when the bill is held up to a light
- Special paper that gives paper money a certain feel

Odd Facts about American Coins and Bills

- Paper money can survive a trip through the laundry because it is actually made of cloth, not paper.

- In most countries, the smaller the coin, the smaller the denomination. In American money, the dime is the smallest coin. Both the penny and nickel are larger in size.

- The Bureau of Engraving and Printing (BEP) prints more than half a billion dollars worth of money every day.

- A stack of dollar bills one mile high would be worth 14.5 million dollars.
- In a pinch, you can use a dollar bill as a ruler, as it is just slightly over six inches long (6.14 inches/15.2 cm).
- The date on paper money doesn't change every year as it does on coins. A new year is printed on paper money only when the Secretary of the Treasury changes or a bill is redesigned.

Money Past, Present, and Future

Over the years, American money has come in many forms. People used to trade furs or beads called wampum instead of money. Early Americans used Spanish gold pieces called *Pieces of Eight* as their currency.

Today, more money is in **circulation** than ever. Still, some people believe that paper money and coins will be replaced by credit cards and other forms of payment in the future. That may happen someday, but for now, paper bills and coins remain an important part of American society.

Glossary

circulation (sur-kyuh-LAY-shun): the amount of bills and coins in use

commemorating (kuh-MEM-uh-rate-ing): remembering and honoring a person or event

counterfeit (KOUN-tur-fit): something that has been made to look like the real thing but is fake, such as counterfeit money

currency (KUR-uhn-see): the form of money used in a country

denomination (di-nom-uh-NAY-shuhn): a value or unit in a system of measurement

mint (MINT): a place where coins are manufactured

monuments (MON-yuh-muhnts): statues, buildings, or other structures that are meant to remind people of an event or person

obverse (OB-vurss): the front of a coin or bill

reverse (ri-VURSS): the back of a coin or bill

security (si-KYOOR-uh-tee): making secure or safe

treasury (TREZH-ur-ee): a government department that is in charge of collecting taxes and managing the public's money

31

Index

Further Reading

Hill, Mary. *Dollars.* Children's Press, 2005.

Robinson, Elizabeth Keeler, *Making Cents.* Tricycle Press, 2008.

Scheunemann, Pam. *Cool Coins.* Checkerboard Books, 2006.

Websites

www.numismatics.org/

www.moneyfactory.gov/

www.usmint.gov/kids/

About the Author

Tim Clifford is an educational writer and the author of many nonfiction children's books. He has two wonderful daughters and two energetic Border Collies that he adopted from a shelter. Tim became a vegetarian because of his love for animals. He is also a computer nut and a sports fanatic. He lives and works in New York City as a public school teacher.